PARENTING TEENS

with

BIPOLAR DISORDER

Helping Your Teen Through Mood Swings with Love and Support

Rosemary E. Walton

Content

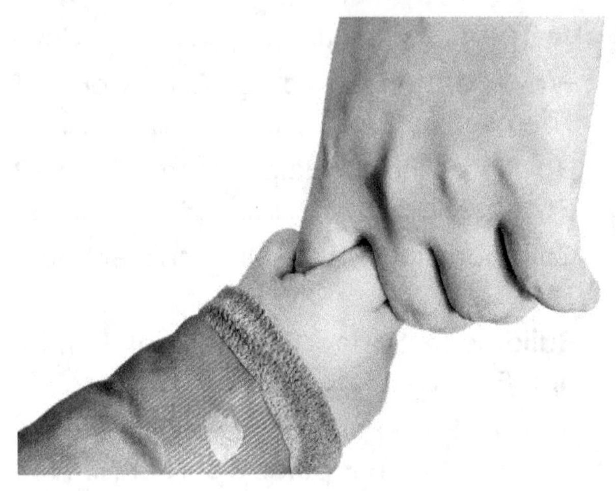

Introduction

Alida always knew that having a teenager would be hard, but she did not know what to do when her son Rodney's moods started to change wildly. Rodney was excited and full of energy as he talked about his big plans for the future. He would stay up late because everything was making him happy. Then, out of the blue, he would become so sad that he could hardly move or talk to anyone. It was hard to keep up with these ups and downs. Rodney was finally told he had bipolar illness after months of not knowing what was wrong.

For Alida, this was both good news and something new to think about. Though she realized her son was struggling, she was not sure how to support him. She did not know what the future held for Rodney and felt his bipolar condition was too much to manage.

How could she help him deal with his feelings? In the long run, would he be okay?

The story of Alida is one that many parents can connect to. There are some hard things about being a parent of a teen with bipolar disorder, but there are also chances to learn, grow, and help your teen in ways that really matter.

Here you will find information on how to help your teen deal with their feelings when they are having bipolar disorder.With this book, Alida and other parents like you will be able to get through the often hard and confusing process of raising a teen with bipolar illness. This guide has the information, support, and tools you need to help your teen deal with their mood swings and live a balanced life, whether they were just identified or you have been on this path for a while.

We will talk about what bipolar illness is and how it affects teens in this book. You will learn useful tips for making your home a safe place that helps your teen handle their feelings, and we will also talk about how important it is to talk to each other and understand each other. This book has all the important steps you and your teen need to take to get better, from getting the right treatment to being there for them at school. For teens with bipolar disorder, it can be hard to raise them. But you can be there for them through the good times and bad with understanding, patience, and the right tools. You will learn that your help and support can make all the difference, just like Alida did with Rodney.

Chapter 1

What Is Bipolar Disorder?

One sign of a mental health condition known as bipolar disorder are extreme mood swings. Your teen might therefore go through manic episodes, or moments when they feel quite euphoric and high, then go through depressed episodes, or times when they feel quite down and sad. These emotional swings much exceed the usual ups and downs youngsters go through.

During manic episodes, your teen can act impulsively, speak too rapidly, or engage in activities they would not usually do. During depressed moments, they could get tired, dejected, and lose interest in usually fun events.

Not only is bipolar disease a valid medical condition; it is not just moodiness. If your teen receives the right direction and help, he or she can manage these changes.

Understanding Bipolar Disorder

The mood, energy, and behavior of someone with bipolar illness change a lot during the day. The changes can be very strong and happen quickly, most of the time without warning. They might feel like anything is possible when they are really happy, excited, or even full of energy. They may jump right into jobs or feel like they can handle anything when these things happen. They might be fine one minute and feel awful the next, leaving them feeling lost, really down, or even sleepy. This change can be hard for everyone, not just the person going through it. The phase with a lot of energy, called mania, really stands out from the phase with low energy, called sadness.

You will not feel this way when your mood changes. These changes are much bigger and can last for days, weeks, or even longer. Teenagers who have bipolar illness may find it hard to go about their daily lives when their moods change this much. Teenagers who are manic may feel too busy, have thoughts that change quickly, and do unsafe things. They might talk a lot and have trouble sleeping. They may choose or make big plans without giving them much thought. Teenagers with this much energy may find it difficult to perform effectively at home, with friends, and at school since they behave in erratic manner.

The teen could feel depressed, exhausted, and unmotivated in this period about the things they typically enjoy. They might modify their eating and sleeping habits, struggle to focus in the classroom, and feel as though they have nothing to contribute or value. Under the worst of circumstances, this can cause them to distance themselves from friends and family. They might even consider injuring or killing themselves.

People of all ages have to be informed about bipolar disease. Parents should thus be aware that the mood fluctuations of their teenagers indicate a major disease rather than only a phase or typical teen behavior. Being a parent can make it difficult to know how to effectively support your teen through ups and downs. Parents might not know how to support their teen in handling emotional fluctuations or feeling anxious about their employment. They may also be concerned about how bipolar disease might impact their family's way of life and their teen's future.

Life can be hard to plan and understand for teens who have bipolar disorder. They might feel alone sometimes because their family and friends might not know what they are going through. They might not be able to control how they feel and act, which could make things tough at school and with other people. It can be hard to take care of someone with bipolar disorder when their symptoms make everyday things feel too much.

To get through this, parents and teenagers alike need understanding and support. Making sure their teen is safe and receives the required treatment mostly relies on parents. Teenagers need resources, understanding, and guidance to handle their issues.

What you need to know about the Two Types: Bipolar I and Bipolar II

Knowing the two forms of bipolar illness—Bipolar I and Bipolar II—you can truly help your teen get through their challenges. Though they impact people in various ways, both kinds have strong mood swings. Knowing their distinctions will enable you to handle their circumstances more sensibly.

People with bipolar I disorder generally experience really significant mood fluctuations. Teenagers suffering from bipolar I will experience at least one hyper episode. During a hyper episode, your teen could act dangerously and feel extremely high and energetic. They may change their thoughts fast, speak rapidly, and take on more than they can manage. They might also engage in risky behaviors such as overspending or making snap decisions devoid of consideration for the future. These manic episodes can become so severe that they interfere with daily activities and your teen could even have to visit a hospital to remain safe and properly manage their symptoms.

Apart from these manic episodes, bipolar I also experiences periods of extreme depression for the individual. Your teen may experience depression, helplessness, or less passion in activities they used to enjoy at these times. They might either sleep too much or have difficulties sleeping. Their appetite can alter and it could be difficult for them to concentrate on homework or other everyday chores. The depressed periods of bipolar I can be equally as disruptive as the manic episodes, therefore affecting their relationships and daily activities. These mood fluctuations are indicators of a major illness that has to be properly treated and understood, not merely typical teenage ups and downs.

Though it has some distinctions, bipolar II disorder is comparable to bipolar I disorder in some respects. Rather than experiencing complete-fledged manic episodes, bipolar II individuals endure what are known as hypomanic episodes. Mania is worse than hypomania. Your teen might still be thrilled and full of energy during a hypomanic period, but not as much as they would in Bipolar I. Though their behavior is not as bad as someone who is manic, they could be more talkative and active. Most of the time, hypomanic episodes are less disruptive and do not produce significant issues requiring hospitalization. It can be difficult for your teen to keep things under control though as they can still affect their attitude and behavior.

Usually severe and lasting longer in Bipolar II than in Bipolar I, these depressive episodes in Bipolar II These phases of depression can be really severe, resulting in a lot of tension and difficulties doing daily tasks. Should this occur, your teen can become rather depressed, quite fatigued, and lose interest in activities they formerly loved. These indicators can make it difficult for teens to excel in daily life, among friends, and in the classroom. Those with bipolar II generally find it simpler to recognize and manage their sad episodes than their hypomanic ones.

Getting your teen the proper support and care depends on knowing the differences between Bipolar I and Bipolar II. Those with bipolar I may require more intense treatment and experience more severe manic episodes. While depressed phases are worse and continue longer, bipolar II includes hypomanic episodes not as severe. This information will enable you to better support your teen in handling their symptoms and grasp what they are going through.

Knowing what type of bipolar disease your teen has will enable you as a parent in several respects. It enables you to identify their symptoms and possible influence on their daily lives. When you are collaborating with medical specialists to create a treatment plan for your teen that matches their requirements, this knowledge is rather crucial. Many times, medication and therapy assist individuals manage both depressed phases and manic or hypomanic episodes.

Understanding the variations between Bipolar I and Bipolar II will also help you manage and get ready for the mood swings of your teen. You can set up routines, make their house a motivating environment, and search for strategies to help them manage their symptoms. Knowing these variations will also enable you to provide your teen the required support and care as well as enable more clear communication with them.

Though the sad periods in Bipolar I and II are distinct and the manic or hypomanic episodes in Bipolar I and II are not as severe, both induce significant mood shifts. Bipolar I suffers from quite severe depressed phases and manic surges. Less terrible hypomanic episodes and more obvious depressed periods define bipolar II. Knowing these variations will help you better assist your teen and cooperate with their healthcare staff to let them lead a balanced and fulfilling existence.

How you can Spot the Signs in Your Teen

Although it can be difficult, determining if your teen is manic or depressed will help you to better grasp their situation. Important components of bipolar disease are both Mania and Depression. Understanding these indicators will enable you to get your teenage teen the correct treatment and support.

If your teen is manic, you could find they seem to be quite active or busy. They can not sleep, hence they remain up late and work on many things at once. Those who experience this could believe they are on an everlasting high. Mania might cause them to also appear overly pleasant, energetic, or even euphoric. Usually not like them, their conversations may be fast, flit from one topic to another, and be unduly optimistic about everything.

Mania might sometimes lead one to act without thinking. Your teen could seem to make hasty decisions or engage in risky behavior. Among the things that might happen are overcommitting oneself, overspending, or acting without thinking through what might happen. Teens who behave this manner might disrupt their own lives as well as that of their surroundings.

They might behave differently during these times than the careful or deliberate person they often are.

Should your teen be experiencing a manic episode, they might also talk more than usual. They could not only talk more but also fast, moving from one idea to the next without pauses. Their increasing conversation could make it difficult for them to remain on subject and could cause more frequent disturbance of others. Since they are always shifting their focus from one subject to another, it can also be difficult for them to focus on careers.

On the other hand, when your teen is depressed, the symptoms are quite different but still very crucial to observe. They could seem as though they are constantly depressed. They are not just experiencing a fleeting mood fluctuation; this melancholy is a deep, long-lasting feeling that can influence all they do. They used to be more engaged in hobbies, social activities, or even their preferred school subjects, but you can find that nowadays they are not as so. Their lack can be quite clear since they could not desire to spend time with friends and relatives or become thrilled about items they used to appreciate.

If your teen is depressed, their sleeping habits might also shift. You may find them struggling to fall asleep, laying awake at night unable to relax, or sleeping excessively, feeling exhausted even after a long night's sleep. These variations in sleep patterns might cause tiredness, affect their mood and capacity to do everyday tasks.

Another indication of despondency is not eating as much. Your teen's weight will show changes whether they consume a lot more or a lot less than usual. Some folks could eat comfort foods more often or might not be as hungry for meals. These dietary modifications could have an impact on their health and help to explain their mental state.

During a depressive episode, your teen can also feel lazy or fatigued. They could claim they are worn out or that they find it difficult to go about daily tasks. When teens feel this weary, they could find it difficult to keep motivated in activities or do well in the classroom. Their difficulty focusing could make it difficult for them to complete their assignments or stay to their objectives.

Sometimes depression causes one to consider more critical issues. Your teen can claim to feel hopeless or to be useless. In the worst of circumstances, people could discuss suicide or self-harm. Should you come across any of these crucial ideas or actions, you should treat them quite seriously and seek assistance immediately.

Knowing these symptoms of mania and despair will help you determine whether your teen suffers with bipolar disease. Observing their behavior and mood swings will help you to better understand their issues and assist them in obtaining the required assistance. Knowing these indicators will enable you to ensure you can act fast should their condition deteriorate and provide better treatment.

Learning how Bipolar Disorder Affects Your Teen's Behavior

Knowing how bipolar illness influences your teen's behaviors will help you support them in the proper manner. Teenagers with bipolar disease may experience significant changes in their mood, behavior, and social interaction. Knowing these consequences will enable you to further help them.

Your teen can behave much differently from their usual manner during a manic episode. They could seem rather eager and have great energy at these times. Their excessively high energy levels could encourage them to start too many jobs at once or take on more than they can handle. Though they may struggle to fall asleep or remain up late, they nonetheless seem to be rather energetic. Their mood could also get really high and they might express too much delight or excitement. They may hop from one topic to another frequently, speak faster than usual, and exude a really good attitude about their aspirations or values.

Your teen might also act without reason during these manic episodes. People may act without really considering the consequences of those actions. They might act in ways that might get them in problems, purchase items they do not need, or take chances. They might not be careful, for instance, when they are around other people, which would cause arguments with friends or relatives. This rage might lead things to go wrong at home or at a school.

They could also have trouble focusing during a manic bout. Their difficulty focusing could make it difficult for them to complete housework or handle other tasks. Their minds are continually running, hence they may not be able to complete one project before beginning another. Their great restlessness could make it difficult for them to make eye contact with others and cause them to become enraged fast when other people move more slowly than they would want.

Your teen behaves differently yet when they are depressed. Depressed people can feel quite lost and hopeless. Your teen could stop engaging in sports, pastimes, or hanging out with friends at these times—activities they used to like. This getaway could make them feel even more alone since they are avoiding social events and spending more time by themselves.

Should your teen be depressed, they could feel quite exhausted or have little energy. Their lack of desire would make it difficult for them to get out of bed or complete daily chores. They might not be able to enjoy the activities they used to and do as well in school due to their diminished energy. Those who believe they are unmotivated and lazy could find daily tasks difficult.

Depression can influence how your teen interacts with others in addition to these variations in activity and energy levels. Responding more aggressively to events that would not typically disturb them, they may grow more irritable or snappier. Their contacts with friends and relatives could become strained. Their mood fluctuations might make maintaining healthy connections difficult, which might cause misinterpretation and conflicts.

Furthermore, influencing your teen's view of themselves is bipolar disease. When they are hyper, they may feel highly confident of themselves and that they cannot lose, which would lead them to engage in more than they can handle. On the other hand, when people are depressed, their sense of self-worth may wane, which would cause them to feel inadequate about themselves or as if they had nothing of value. These shifts in their self-perception could influence their behavior and drive in many different settings, including social events and their place of education.

These behavioral changes should be observed so that you may provide your teen the correct assistance. Knowing when they are hyper or depressed will help you to further satisfy their requirements. During manic episodes, setting boundaries and supporting them in work planning can help prevent overwhelming them. Giving them some assistance and keeping them occupied with activities can be quite beneficial during depressed episodes.

By always observing and analyzing these behavioral changes, you can assist your teen negotiate the challenges of bipolar illness. Their capacity to handle their illness and lead a contented life can be much enhanced by a safe and caring environment as well as by recognition of the highs and lows they experience.

Chapter 2

Supporting Your Teen with bipolar disorder at Home

A few easy steps can help you help your teen with bipolar illness at home. Your teen may feel more stable and sure of what will happen if they stick to a daily plan. Make sure they get enough sleep, eat well, and exercise regularly. These things will help keep their energy and mood in check. Set up a safe space where they feel comfortable talking about how they feel and encourage them to do so. Stay cool and understanding when they are having mood swings. When they are hysterical, help them control their energy, and when they are down, be there for them. Make rules that are clear, fair, and take into account their changing feelings. Be flexible. You can make your home a better place for your teen to deal with their bipolar disease by sticking to routines, encouraging healthy habits, and letting them talk to you freely. Your help and understanding can make a big difference in how well they can deal with things and feel better.

How You Can Create a Steady Routine for Your Teen

Giving your teen a consistent schedule will assist them manage bipolar disease among other things. Teenagers who experience the emotional upheavals and mood swings associated with bipolar illness could find great benefit from a disciplined daily schedule since it provides stability and consistency. This essay addresses why consistent practice can make a significant difference as well as how you might help it to be effective.

The most crucial thing is to schedule consistent waking and bed-going hours. Establishing a consistent sleeping schedule for your teen will help to maintain their body clock in sync, facilitating adequate rest. Your teen should develop consistent sleeping habits since sleep disorders can aggravate mood swings and complicate their handling of their emotions. On weekends as well, your teen should aim to get up and go to bed at the same time every day. This regularity provides you a sense of rhythm and normalcy in addition to improved sleeping quality.

Meal times should also be decided upon and easily recalled. Establishing breakfast, lunch, and supper timings will enable you to keep fit and create a more ordered surroundings. Regular meal times will enable your teen to acquire the nutrients they require, thereby enhancing their energy and mood. Cooking meals together and planning help people feel more engaged in their everyday life and provide a sense of routine.

Your daily calendar ought to include scheduled hours for leisure and study. Establishing frequent study sessions and breaks will enable your teen to manage their homework and provide them time for leisure and hobbies. Maintaining balance between work and leisure will help you prevent anxiety and emotions of excessive busyness, which might cause mood swings. Creating a visual calendar of daily activities will enable your teen to make wise use of their time and know what to expect.

Apart from these organized activities, your teen should develop a regular workout routine in line with their lifestyle. Natural mood enhancement and reduction of anxiety and worry might come from regular workout.

Encourage your teen to engage in physical activities they enjoy—walking, playing sports, or attending fitness courses. Regular exercise lowers mood swings, so enhancing your mental health in addition to your physical condition.

Just as vital is scheduling time to unwind and look after oneself. Help your teen choose activities that will help them to feel serene and quiet. Reading, listening to music, meditating or practicing awareness, or engaging in leisurely creative activity are a few instances of this. Especially when they are feeling emotionally or psychologically overwhelmed, scheduling time for these pursuits can be rather significant for their daily life.

Establishing a consistent schedule also enables one to be able to adjust as required. While consistency is crucial, one also needs to be aware of when adjustments are required. For instance, you could have to modify your teen's schedule to match their requirements if they are having a very difficult day. This indicates that you know and support your teen; they will feel safe knowing they may alter their pattern as needed without losing its general structure.

Regular family events and consistent time spent with one another might also assist to keep things in line. Trips, game evenings, and family dinners all help to bring people together and provide encouragement. These common events not only strengthen your family but also provide your teen with stability and normalcy, which would assist them manage their bipolar condition.

Monitoring the schedule and making necessary adjustments is also quite vital. See how the process is working for you and be ready to make adjustments when needed.

Regularly check in with your teen to find out how they are managing their plan and whether they believe they require more assistance with any one thing. This constant contact guarantees that the practice suits their current demands and operates as expected.

Establishing a regular habit ensures that you sleep enough, eat at consistent times, study and play at designated times, engage in some exercise, and unwind. While consistency is vital, so is adaptability and paying attention to what your teen needs. Establishing and modifying a disciplined daily schedule will provide your teen the consistency and predictability required to manage their bipolar illness. Their general health and happiness depend on their feeling of safety and grounding, hence this consistent schedule not only improves their mental health but also helps them in these aspects.

How Sleep, Food, and Daily Habits Affect Your Teen's Mood

Particularly if your teen is managing bipolar illness, their sleep patterns, eating habits, and daily schedule dramatically affect their mood and general well-being. These elements interact and greatly affect your teen's daily feelings and behavior. Being aware of how each one affects your teen will help you to provide them the assistance they require and create a safe surroundings promoting emotional equilibrium.

Let us now consider sleep. Controlling mood depends on regular sleep, especially for youth with bipolar illness. One must keep a regular sleeping schedule. This means setting consistent wake-up and bedtimes—including on weekends. For your adolescent to maintain internal clock stability—which is necessary to minimize mood swings and preserve emotional balance—a regular sleep regimen is Developing a regular nighttime schedule could help greatly minimize mood swings and heightened irritability brought on by disturbed sleep.

Furthermore crucial is creating a calm sleeping environment. Before bed, cut your teen's screen and technology intake so their bedroom is a peaceful place for sleep. The blue light of these devices can throw off the body's melatonin synthesis, a hormone regulating sleep. A peaceful, dark room will help your teen fall asleep and stay asleep for longer. Developing calm before-bed rituals including reading or relaxing music will help you relax and be ready for a nice night's sleep.

Let us now talk about diet. Teenagers' energy and attitude are much influenced by the food they eat. A balanced diet supports both general mental health and a steady mood. Encourage your teenager to have a variety of foods including lean meats, nutritious grains, fruits, vegetables, and good fats. These meals' key nutrients support brain function and mood control. Foods heavy in omega-3 fatty acids, such as flaxseeds and salmon, can help one feel better, for example. Similarly, the complex carbs in whole grains help to maintain steady blood sugar levels, therefore reducing mood swings.

Furthermore, it is important to restrict specific foods and beverages that might negatively affect mood. Sugary foods and drinks high in caffeine, such coffee and energy drinks, can rapidly change blood sugar levels, which can cause mood swings and agitation. By helping your teen to cut back on these drugs, you can help them to have a more constant attitude and energy level. Getting your teen involved in the meal planning and cooking process will help them to learn about good eating and pique their interest in their diet. It gives people an opportunity to connect and discuss how their food choices impact their feelings.

Physical activity is yet another crucial element in regulating general health and mood. Regular exercise has been shown to produce endorphins, naturally occurring mood boosters. Encouragement of physical activities your teen enjoys can help them to develop a more regular and enjoyable habit in their lives. Whether your teenager likes swimming, dancing, athletics, or just walks, it is crucial to find activities they look forward to. Regular exercise enhances mood, reduces stress, and encourages better sleep among other things.

There are various ways to include physical activity into your teen's regular calendar. Set aside time every week for exercise; find methods to start moving when you go about daily activities like walking or biking to school. By helping your teen develop reasonable fitness goals and identify interests, exercise could start to be a regular and fun activity in their life. Even daily chores requiring movement, such as cleaning or hobbies, can help individuals remain active and support mood control.

Establishing a plan including regular physical activity, a healthy diet, and consistent sleep will help your teen live in a supporting environment. Maintaining consistency in these areas helps to support stability and predictability, which is very helpful for the management of bipolar illness. Although occasionally deviating from the plan is normal, maintaining general consistency will help your teen feel stable and safe.

You really should be involved in your teen's daily schedule. Their welfare depends on you since you help teens to keep a consistent sleeping schedule, plan and prepare healthy meals, and participate in enjoyable physical activities. Establishing a regulated and motivating environment comprising five key elements will help your teen to better control their general health and mood.

Control of bipolar illness begins with a great emphasis on diet, exercise, and sleep. A balanced diet supports mental health; regular exercise enhances emotional well-being; and a consistent sleeping schedule helps to calm mood. While helping your teen overcome the challenges presented by bipolar illness, your proactive support in these areas encourages a more balanced, healthy lifestyle.

How to Encourage Your Teen to Talk Openly About Their Feelings

Encouragement of your teen with bipolar illness on open communication of their emotions is absolutely vital. Open communication with them not only clarifies their feelings but also provides the means required for them to tackle their issues. Establishing a strong relationship and enhancing your teen's general health depend on a safe environment where they may share their emotions.

Ensuring that everyone in your house supports you and refutes judgment of you is very crucial. Your teen should be able to tell you how they feel free from thinking about being judged or turned down. Reiter to them your constant listening to what they have to say. Your encouraging comments should originate from the heart and underline that you are always there for them and that their emotions are natural. Establishing trust is quite crucial since it increases the likelihood of your teen sharing their most private thoughts and emotions with you.

Getting people to interact with one another depends on active listening in great part. Pay great attention while your youngster shares with you their feelings. This means stashing computers and phones and concentrating just on the discourse. One should not dismiss them or respond immediately. Let them express anything they wish to and chat at their own speed. If you show that you understand and care for their emotions, it can make a great difference. Tell them you are here for them and that you understand how vital what they are going through is. This will improve their mood.

Your teen may find it difficult to approach someone they do not know. In these contexts, it can assist to present yourself in several ways. Writing is a more indirect approach for your teen to express their ideas and convey what they wish to. Instruct teens to start a notebook in which they may record their emotions, ideas, and actions. Writing helps teens better grasp what is on their minds and provides a safe forum for them to express it. If they allow, there may be instances when you review their book with them. If you do this, you will be more suited to help them and grasp what they are going through.

Two artistic or musical pursuits that could enable your teen to express their emotions are creating art or music. Being creative can enable individuals to manage their emotions and communicate about their experiences in a way that words could not be able to. By satisfying their needs and expressing interest in their creations, you can enable them to achieve their objectives. This not only motivates your teen to speak up but also demonstrates your concern for their mental health and respect of their speaking abilities.

Frequent contact with people is another effective approach to start conversations. Establishing frequent occasions to discuss your teen's emotions can enable you to keep in contact and strengthen your bond. These check-ins can occur shortly before bed, during family dinner, or when the house is quiet. It becomes natural when someone constantly expresses their opinions in the same manner. Furthermore, it provides your teen with the opportunity to share their ideas and emotions, which could be comforting and encouraging.

Discuss emotions with an open mind and a thirst to learn always. If your teen says anything you find incomprehensible or disagreeable, it is crucial to pay attention to them. Inquire of them open-ended inquiries like "Can you help me understand what has been upsetting you?" to get them to discuss their feelings more. Using this approach will enable you and your teen to get closer and demonstrate your sincere curiosity in their life.

Including additional loving individuals into your teen's life might also be beneficial. This might be a friend, a family member, or a reputable mental health professional. Hearing many points of view or discussing your concerns with someone unrelated to you occasionally helps more than anything else. Finding someone your teen can rely on to communicate will enable them to have more means to express their emotions and feel more emotionally steady.

Keeping your cool throughout these presentations is also really crucial. When your teen tells you about their difficulties, it is natural for you to worry or feel afraid; but, it is crucial to keep cool and patient. Control yourself. Losing your temper might cause your youngster to refuse to interact with you going forward. Their impression of free and honest communication with you is enhanced by your calm and helpful attitude, which helps them to relax about possible outcomes.

Encouragement of honest conversation about emotions goes beyond merely addressing current issues. Part of it is scheduling frequent talks where your teen feels comfortable sharing their emotions. Creating a setting that values honest communication, getting in contact with your teen in several ways, and routinely checking in with them will help your teen feel safer and more understood.

You have to be proactive and inspire your teen with bipolar illness to be able to manage their symptoms by talking about their emotions. By listening to your teen with empathy, letting them use several kinds of communication, and scheduling frequent periods for conversation, you may help them to manage their emotions. Their physical and emotional health depend much on this kind of support, which also strengthens your bond with them.

What You Should Do During Your Teen's Mood Swings

If your teen has bipolar disorder and is having mood swings, being calm and helpful can have a big effect on their health and how they deal with these hard times. To help someone handle their condition well and give them the right support, you need to know what to do during both manic and depressive phases.

During a manic phase, your teen may have a lot of energy, act without thinking, and be in a very good mood. They might feel antsy and overly active at this point, which could make them take on too many jobs or do dangerous things. Making sure they remain safe and guiding them in using their energy in a positive way falls on you as a parent. First, make the rules clear and easy to follow. This means setting limits on what they can do and helping them organize their work into jobs that are both important and doable. It is important to keep them focused on useful jobs and stop them from letting their energy make them make hasty choices.

Helping them break down big jobs into smaller, easier-to-handle steps is a good way to keep their energy in check. This can help them stay on track with their tasks and keep them from feeling too busy. For instance, if they are excited about starting a new project, help them make an organized plan with clear due dates and goals. This helps them make good use of their energy without getting too confused or stressed out.

Also, it is important to keep an eye on their safety when they are manic. If they are doing dangerous things or making snap choices, step in gently to stop them from hurting themselves. As an example, this could mean putting more limits on what they can do or being there to help them relax so they can make better decisions. Being understanding and helpful during these times can help them feel more grounded and safe, which can make the manic phase less intense.

My teen may have a bad mood, lose drive, and have trouble doing everyday things when they are depressed. This might make it hard for them to stick to their habits or enjoy the things they normally enjoy. Your help during these tough times is very important for keeping them feeling normal and at ease. Encourage them gently to stick to their daily schedules, even if they do not want to. Having a routine can give you order and stability, which are very important when you are depressed.

Small, doable steps can make a big difference when they are encouraged. Instead of pushing them to finish everything they need to do in one day, set small goals that they can reach. Say, if they are having trouble getting out of bed, tell them to start with something easy like taking a shower or eating. Getting them to do bigger jobs little by little can help them feel like they are back to normal.

Always be positive and remind them of their skills and accomplishments. Tell them that you are there for them and that your efforts are valuable, even if they do not seem interested or willing to help. Even when things are hard, giving them compliments and gentle reminders of what they can do can help improve their self-esteem and motivation.

Keeping the lines of conversation open during depressive episodes is an important part of making the environment supportive. Your teen should be able to talk about how they feel, but you should also respect their need for room. Do not push them to talk if they are not ready. Respect their limits. Rather, tell them you are here for them always and that you are available whenever they wish to talk.

Help with everyday tasks can be just as helpful as mental support. Help your teen with everyday jobs that may seem too hard when they are depressed. This could mean helping them with chores around the house, setting up their plan, or reminding them of important events. Your support in person can help them deal with some of their problems and keep up with their routine.

It is also a smart idea to monitor any changes in their behavior or mood closely. Keeping track of their mood fluctuations in a diary will enable them to identify the triggers for their bipolar disease and learn better management techniques.
Tell their doctor about any observations you have to make sure that their treatment plan is still right and working.

Remember that you should be kind and patient with them. Mood swings can be hard for both you and your teen, but it is important to stay helpful and understanding. During hyper episodes, make sure they are safe and help them use their energy in a healthy way. During times of depression, help them stay on track with their daily tasks and find comfort by giving them gentle support and encouragement.

You can help your teen deal with their mood swings by giving them structure, making sure they are safe, and giving them mental support. You can really help them get through the ups and downs of bipolar disorder if you understand what they need at different times and react with empathy and useful information. Your steady support and calm attitude can make a big difference in how well they can deal with their situation and stay healthy overall.

How to Set Fair Rules and Limits for Your Teen

Setting clear rules and expectations for everyone helps your teen with bipolar illness feel safe and supported. The best way to put these thoughts into action is spelled out in this short outline.

First, get your teen involved in the process of making the rules. Have a conversation with them about what they think is fair and how long they can concentrate. Participating in the creation of rules will help people understand them better and make them more likely to be followed.

Make the rules clearer and easier to understand. Instead of saying something unclear like "Do your homework better," give clear instructions like "Dedicate 30 minutes to your schoolwork every evening after dinner." Guidelines make it clear what you expect from your teen, clearing up any confusion.

It is important to be consistent. Hold people accountable for following the rules you have set. If a limit is set for 10 p.m., it must be followed every time and not be extended sometimes. The set rules that are always followed give your teen a sense of comfort and predictability.

Make sure that the rules can be followed and are reasonable. You should think about how your teen feels when you set limits. To keep them from taking on too much, set tighter limits if they show a lot of energy during a manic phase. Make sure the standards are not too hard to meet or too discouraging for people who are depressed. It is important that the rules are flexible, but they also need to be fair and easy to understand.

What happens next must make sense and have something to do with the crime. If you think your teen might not follow their bedtime, you might want to set a temporary earlier curfew. Give a short explanation of what will happen and make sure that people follow through if they break the rules. This helps your teen understand what will happen if they do not follow the rules and encourages them to do so.

Use positive encouragement to get people to behave in a good way. You should praise your teen when they make good decisions or follow the rules. This could mean giving short words of support or small rewards, like more screen time. When their efforts are noticed, it makes them feel better and encourages them to keep following the rules.

Maintain the talk with your teen about the rules. Regularly ask them what they think about the rules and see if any changes need to be made. This shows that you are willing to change to better fit their needs and that you value their opinions.

Deal with the problem with kindness and help, while still sticking to your values. Keep your cool and focus on coming up with answers with your teen as a group when they break the rules instead of just punishing them. By knowing why they are breaking the rules and working together to solve the problem, you can build a sense of support and motivation.

It is very important to find a mix between fair rules and giving help. Including your teen in setting rules, being clear about what is expected of them, giving fair punishments, and using positive reinforcement will help create a stable environment that is good for managing bipolar illness. You can help them better control their feelings and actions by being open and communicating clearly. By showing empathy, you want to make your home a place where your teen feels safe and supported.

Chapter 3

Getting the Right Help and Treatment for Your Teen with Bipolar Disorder

Finding the correct treatment and support for your teen with bipolar illness is rather crucial since their well-being depends much on it. The first step is to find a reputable counselor or doctor who actually understands how to assist teenagers with bipolar illness. Medication can truly enable your teen to better manage their symptoms and strike some equilibrium in their mood. Knowing how these drugs operate and keeping contact with your doctor regarding any side effects you could have is quite crucial. Discussing treatment can be quite beneficial for your family as well as your teen. Your teen would benefit much from learning some coping mechanisms and controlling their condition; family therapy greatly improves household communication and support. Following the treatment plan is absolutely crucial, hence even small encouragement for your teen and putting up some reminders can make a great difference. Along the road, there may be some difficulties; but, working with your healthcare team will enable you to address them and provide your teen with the greatest assistance available.

Finding the Right Doctor or Counselor for Your Teen

Finding the correct help for your teen with bipolar disorder starts with a crucial first step determining which healthcare provider has the knowledge and experience to properly treat the illness. You want a professional who might be a counselor, clinical psychologist, or psychiatrist. The crucial component is to identify someone who has expertise with teenagers and truly understands their condition, particularly with regard to mood disorders including bipolar illness. Teens experience some quite unusual emotional and developmental difficulties, hence it is quite vital to choose someone who not only gets the disorder but also the ups and downs of being a teenager.

First of all, you might find it wise to contact the main care physician for your teen. Usually, they may provide some excellent advice or refer you to local experts who truly understand how to manage bipolar illness. Getting in touch with nearby mental health groups is another excellent suggestion. Many times, they have lists of experts emphasizing on treating teenagers with mood issues. Support groups for families dealing with bipolar illness can be a wonderful tool for locating medical professionals who have changed things for others in similar circumstances.

Having some particular questions ready is a good idea when you first begin meeting with possible psychologists, doctors, or counselors. This will enable you to determine whether they meet the requirements of your teenage teen. Given especially in teenagers, one of the first questions you would want to inquire is their level of experience treating bipolar illness. Teenagers with bipolar disorder may exhibit distinct symptoms than adults, hence having a physician who recognizes those variations can greatly influence your teen's course of therapy.

Why then not find out how they usually approach treatment? While some experts might stress therapy or perhaps combine both approaches, others could want to regulate medications. Understanding their philosophy and approach to bipolar illness will enable you to determine whether it aligns with your values and goals for the treatment of your teen. While some families would prefer a more all-encompassing approach including lifestyle changes, mindfulness methods, or family counseling, others could find it simpler to follow a treatment plan combining medication and cognitive-behavioral therapy.

Finding out how they relate, especially with teenagers is quite crucial. Teens are experiencing a very significant period in their life, hence it is rather crucial to choose a professional who can relate to them and interact effectively. Your expertise working with teens intrigues me. How do you approach those difficult talks? How do you ensure they feel heard and understood using various approaches? The course of treatment might be much improved if your teen visits a therapist or doctor they truly connect with.

One further crucial consideration is how the healthcare provider involves the family into the treatment process. Not only can bipolar illness affect the person; it can also profoundly affect the dynamic of the entire family. Family therapy is increasingly included into treatment strategies by many experts, and it can truly help. This kind of therapy may truly help you and your family understand what your teen is going through, how to best support them, and how to manage the ups and downs bipolar disease can bring into family life.

Additionally very crucial is ensuring your teen feels comfortable with their healthcare professional. The way your teen receives treatment depends much on their relationship with their therapist, doctor, or counselor. Find out from your teen how they view the professional you are considering. Do they feel as though they understand? Do they believe their issues are given importance? Your teen is far more likely to participate in their treatment and follow advice when they have a strong connection and trust with their healthcare professional.

Treatment will start once you have identified the appropriate healthcare provider, but that marks only the beginning of your road. Long-term, bipolar disorder is something that persists and requires constant work, some adjustments along the road, and a good support system. Most likely, your doctor will team with your teen to develop a treatment plan. To assist stabilize their mood and increase their general well-being, this approach probably calls for controlling drugs, therapy, and certain lifestyle adjustments. Maintaining open lines of contact with your healthcare practitioner can help you to monitor your development and, should necessary, modify the treatment plan.

Finding the correct assistance for your teen is only the beginning; yet, it is a very crucial first step to ensure they receive the treatment required to manage their illness. Helping your teen with bipolar illness can be quite a trip, and indeed, it does present difficulties. However, there is plenty of cause for hope regarding a better, more secure future for your teen with the correct professional support and loving family. Your teen can absolutely learn to control their bipolar illness and lead a balanced, happy life with some patience and determination with the correct therapy plan.

Understanding Medicines and How They Can Help Your Teen

Managing bipolar disease depends on drugs, which also significantly affect your teen's daily life. You can better help your teen if you know how these medicines work and what part they play in therapy.

Medication-taking bipolar teenagers help to better control their daily problems and mood. Most often, these treatments contain antidepressants, mood stabilizers and antipsychotics. Also there are effects from different medications, hence it could take a few tries to find the one that fits your teen the most.

First thing those with bipolar disease should take is a mood stabilizer. Their value stems from their ability to reduce the fluctuations in manic and sad episodes. Two rather popular mood stabilizers are lithium and valproate. By regulating the molecules in your brain, lithium helps to maintain your mood steady. On the other side, your teen will have to get frequent blood tests to monitor their lithium levels and ensure the medication is acting as it ought to.

One alternative with identical effect as lithium is valproate. The doctor might prescribe this medication to your teen instead of lithium if valproate helps with their issues or if adverse effects from lithium create concern. Every teen is unique, hence you should be aware of what your teen needs.

Another class of drugs used to treat bipolar illness are antipsychotics. Sometimes they are recommended to treat severe mania or depression symptoms not responding to mood stabilizers by themselves. Antipsychotics help to regulate excessive mood swings, hallucinations, or delusions.

Their actions guide the chemical messengers in the brain, therefore controlling mood. Among the typically used antipsychotics for bipolar disorder are quetiapine, risperidone, and olanzapine. Although certain drugs can be rather successful, side effects including weight gain, fatigue, or changes in appetite could develop.

Sometimes, especially when antipsychotics and mood stabilizers are insufficient, antidepressants are used to lessen depressed symptoms. Antidepressants boost energy levels and let one feel better. Still, they should be used carefully since occasionally they aggravate mood swings or lead to manic episodes. These drugs ought to be taken under competent medical advice and constantly watched.

Knowing the side effects to be on alert for and how a new drug your teen starts works is absolutely vital. Every medication has adverse effects, hence what benefits one person might not be able to aid another. While some side effects—such as a slight stomach trouble or drowsiness—are brief and mild, others could be more important and influence weight or mood. Tell their doctor any side effects your teen has; modifications in the drug or dosage could be needed.

One has to regularly consult a doctor to make any necessary adjustments and monitor the effectiveness of the medicine. These visits help the doctor evaluate how well the medication is working and whether side effects are starting to show. The healthcare team for your teen may adjust the dosage or medications depending on how your teenager reacts to treatment.

Apart from medication, a family environment with support can greatly help your teen to manage their bipolar illness. Encourage your young person to be open about their emotional condition and to follow their prescription schedule. Setting a calendar will help your teen remember to consistently take their prescription.

You should also maintain open channels of contact with the teenage healthcare practitioner. Discuss any fears you have about the drugs or how they influence your teen's attitude and behavior. Your awareness and involvement will help the doctor to make better informed treatment plan decisions.

While finding the right medication for your teen with bipolar disease takes time and effort, this is vitally essential for managing their condition. Knowing how every type of medication works and planning regular visits can assist to ensure your teen receives the best available treatment. Working with your healthcare team and supporting your teen through their therapy can help them far more to have a balanced and stable existence.

The Benefits of Therapy for Your Teen and Your Family

This is fantastic for the whole family as well as for your youngster suffering from bipolar disease. You have to go beyond merely discussing your difficulties. Along with learning new skills and making relationships, you have to learn how to manage the problems bipolar illness raises. Consider more how therapy might benefit your teen and every member of your family.

Your teen can work through their thoughts and emotions in this secure environment. Having a specialist to consult will enable your teen to grasp the reasons behind their unusual ideas and emotions. Counselors can teach your teen practical methods that would enable them to handle their stress, mood swings, and daily problems. They can also guide your teen in seeing early on mood swings and acting to halt them before they develop more severe.

One quite effective kind of treatment is cognitive behavioral therapy (CBT). Cognitive behavioral therapy (CBT) seeks to eradicate negative behaviors of thought and action. Teaching a mentally ill youngster how to identify and challenge their negative ideas, find better solutions to their issues, and have a more optimistic view of life generally will help them. It allows your teen more control over their behavior and reactions, thereby enabling them to better handle daily events.

Interpersonal and social rhythm treatment, or IPSRT, is another interesting method to treat bipolar disease. This kind of treatment aims to create habits and strengthen relationships. Those with bipolar disease could find it challenging to keep their schedules, which would increase their mood swings. The IPSRT assists your youngster to have daily life in order and to keep solid relationships. Both of these enable people to feel a lot better and maintain their mood. Getting support from friends and relatives is also quite vital for recovery. It affects every bipolar sufferer as well as their families. Every member of the family can visit therapy together to share how the scenario makes them feel. Talking to each other more readily, knowing what your teen is going through, and working together can help you to make your house a caring and safe place. Less conflict and tension will enable everyone to assist one another with this kind of caring through trying circumstances.

It will enable you to better assist your teen and help you to know why they behave the way they do. You might be in conflict with your teen. The therapist can assist you in setting reasonable boundaries, calming down you, and discovering healthier approaches to manage emotions and stress. You are free to express your concerns and emotions without thinking about judgment. This strengthens relationships inside families and facilitates better understanding among people.

Therapy helps your teen address current issues and prepare for ones that might surface in the future. Seeing a therapist will help your teen discover new, long-lasting coping mechanisms for their bipolar illness and stress, therefore enhancing their quality of life. These abilities will enable individuals not only to manage their illness but also other problems arising in their life.

One advantage of treatment is that it benefits for a long period. Your teen can keep in contact with these sites and discuss their development as well as adjust their treatment plan if required. Your teen could believe they have more control over their lives and that constant help helps them feel better.

Family therapy brings happiness and usefulness into the house. If the family knew what bipolar illness is and how it impacts individuals and improved their communication skills, they would get along better. Following family therapy, every member of the family feels less isolated and more linked. The family also is less stressed and performs better collectively.

Therapy offers several ways to benefit your teen and your whole family. It provides your teen with a safe environment in which to discuss their emotions, discover fresh approaches to deal with problems, and improve their bipolar illness management. Family therapy not only makes the house a more pleasant environment but also helps individuals understand and communicate with one another better. This will enable your family and your teen to manage their bulimia better and lead more useful, balanced lives.

Helping Your Teen Stick to Their Treatment Plan

Effective management of bipolar illness and guarantee of your teen's well-being depend on their following of their treatment plan.

Bipolar illness calls for a disciplined and dedicated attitude, hence your teen's staying on track depends much on your assistance. This entails motivating people to keep daily routines, go to therapy sessions, and follow their treatment plan—which usually calls for taking medications as directed.

Treatment must be consistent since it helps regulate symptoms and manages mood swings. Your teen's stability and general quality of life will much improve if they follow their treatment plan. Still, following a treatment plan might be difficult at times; so, support and understanding are rather important.

First of all, your teen should be urged to follow their prescription exactly. The mainstay of bipolar disease treatment are medications, which help to control symptoms and steady mood fluctuations. Help your youngster realize that their therapy depends critically on these drugs and that skipping doses can cause problems. To help your teen remember, schedule a daily medication taking schedule whereby they can easily recall. To aid with tracking, you might set reminders on your phone or utilize a pill organizer.

At home, set up a disciplined space that fits their treatment plan. Create a regular daily schedule including defined times for waking up, getting ready for bed, and other daily tasks. A consistent schedule will assist your teen feel more grounded and less effective fluctuations have an impact on. This arrangement not only helps them with their prescription regimen but also gives their lives normalcy and predictability.

Another absolutely vital component of the therapeutic schedule is showing up for appointments. Therapy guides your teen toward improved understanding of their situation, coping mechanisms, and addressing any problems that surface. Motivational tools for helping your teen control their bipolar illness include therapy. Should they be reluctant to show up for meetings, gently remind them of the advantages and assist in determining how to make the encounter more pleasant. You might, for instance, reassure them about the therapy process or discuss what they want to talk about to assist them get ready for sessions.

Consider employing reminders and tracking devices to guarantee your teen shows up for their visits and follows their treatment plan. Medication schedules, therapy sessions, and any other significant chore connected to their treatment can be tracked on a calendar or smartphone. Setting up a visual plan or using a reminder system that lets your teen know when their prescription or appointment is due helps some families.

Also crucial is honest communication with your teen on their treatment. Help them to see the reason for their drugs and treatments as well as how these elements cooperate to control their symptoms. This information can inspire them to follow their schedule and recognize the worth of their treatment. Steer clear of too aggressive or critical behavior; instead, provide encouragement and support. Your teen's perspective of their treatment and their readiness to follow the plan will be much influenced by your attitude.

Should your teen find it difficult to follow their treatment plan, gently and constructively discuss the problem. Talk about any challenges they might be having, picking their medication or showing up for therapy; then, together, try to discover answers. If they struggle to remember to take their prescription, for instance, look at other reminder systems or approaches that might be more suited for them.

Recall that controlling bipolar illness is an ongoing journey with ups and downs along the road. Be understanding and patient; know that your assistance is much valued under trying circumstances. Celebrate minor achievements and improvement in their therapy; keep motivating and using positive reinforcement.

Helping your teen follow their treatment plan calls for establishing a disciplined and orderly atmosphere, motivating adherence to medicine and therapy, and using reminders and tracking devices. Your teen's capacity to properly control their bipolar illness will be much improved by open discussion about the value of their treatment combined with mild support and understanding. Your teen will be far more balanced and fulfilled if you remain involved and proactive, supporting them to live such a life.

Dealing with Challenges in Treatment

Supporting your teen depends on addressing difficulties in treatment for bipolar illness. Medication and treatment can have their own set of challenges even if they might be quite successful. These obstacles could include adverse effects from drugs or trouble following the treatment plan, both of which could influence how well your teen controls their illness.

Managing side effects from drugs is one typical difficulty. Although drugs are absolutely essential for controlling symptoms and regulating mood, occasionally they have negative side effects. From minor problems like tiredness or nausea to more major concerns like weight gain or mood swings, these side effects could range. Should your teen have side effects, it is crucial to discuss these with their doctor right away. To control the negative effects, the healthcare professional could advise changing the dosage, moving to another medicine, or considering further therapies. Open and honest communication with the doctor helps ensure that any problems are treated rapidly and effectively, which can help your teen have a better whole treatment experience.

It is also important to understand that occasionally your teen may object to their treatment plan or battle with their symptoms. For you and your teen especially, this may be rather difficult and aggravating. Treatment resistance could result from a range of elements, including lack of motivation, side effects from drugs, or overwhelm by the condition. Maintaining understanding and patience is absolutely vital during these times. Your teen may require more support and reassurance to keep on target with their therapy. Talk freely about their emotions and worries, then cooperate to identify answers that would help the therapy process be more under control.

Dealing with these obstacles calls for careful coordination with your teen's healthcare team. Doctors, therapists, and counselors among other members of the healthcare team can offer insightful direction and encouragement. Based on how your teen is reacting to therapy and medication, they can help modify the course of treatment.

This could call for trying several drugs, changing dosages, or including other therapeutic modalities. Maintaining a constant communication with the healthcare staff guarantees that your teen's treatment stays successful and that any problems are resolved right away.

Apart from problems connected to medications, following the treatment plan can sometimes prove challenging. This could entail remembering to routinely take prescriptions, show up for therapy, or follow through with lifestyle adjustments that enhance their general well-being. Using tracking tools or creating reminders could help your teen remain on target. To monitor therapy visits and medication schedules, for instance, you might use a daily planner or a smartphone app. A lot can change if you help your teen to be proactive about their therapy and guide them in forming positive habits.

Remember that controlling bipolar illness is a long-term endeavor and that difficulties are natural on this road. As a supporting parent, you help your teen negotiate these challenges while keeping a good attitude. Celebrate little successes and advancement, and provide hope in trying circumstances. Helping your teen control their illness and have a happy life depends mostly on your support and engagement.

You greatly help your teen to be generally successful in managing bipolar illness by keeping updated about their therapy and acting early to address any difficulties. Work closely with doctors, keep lines of open contact, and help your teen follow their treatment plan. By your commitment and empathy, you enable your youngster to live in a more consistent and encouraging environment, thereby improving their capacity to control their condition.

Chapter 4

Talking and Listening to Your Teen

Open communication with your teenage teen about bipolar illness is crucial. Find a quiet moment to convey your love and encouragement. Simply said, bipolar disorder affects mood and causes periods of great activity and extreme melancholy. Let your teen be honest about not knowing everything and ask questions. Learn together from these events. Give your teen your whole attention; consider their emotions; try not to interrupt. This develops trust and shows you concern. Dealing with tough subjects like safety or drugs need composure. Express worries with "I" words, and always wrap your talks with comfort. If your teen mentions suicide or self-harm, treat it seriously and get right away treatment. Developing a close relationship requires consistency, respect of privacy, sharing of your experiences, and celebration of their development. Provide them with coping mechanisms and provide a positive surroundings to assist in management of their illness.

How You Can Effectively Talk About Bipolar Disorder with Your Teen

Managing their bipolar illness will depend on open and helpful communication with your teen. If you wish to support your teen through their issues, you should approach these conversations carefully, respectfully, and clearly. Here's how to schedule these conversations such that you might most assist and support them.

Choose a moment when your teen and you are both calm and ready for conversation. Do not bring up the topic when they are under a lot of stress or have a negative attitude since it may aggravate their anxiety or protection mechanism. Choose a moment when you won't be disturbed and can have a private talk.

Tell them first how much you value and care for them. Tell your teen you will always be there for them regardless of anything. Talk about bipolar illness using simple, age-appropriate terminology that makes sense. Emphasize on what it is and how it influences them. One approach to phrase it is "bipolar disease modifies how your brain governs your mood". This means that you could have mania—that is, moments when you are really excited and full of energy—and depression—that is, times when you are quite sad or weary. Remember that this is a medical problem; you have no responsibility for it. It does not make you less valued personally or change your identity. This approach eliminates guilt or responsibility and encourages things to return to normal.

Your teenage teen should be urged to probe their circumstances. They most certainly have many questions and concerns. By showing that you are ready to discuss things, you will help them to relax and feel as though you are attentive. Own the reality that you are not knowing everything. Although you still have questions about some things, you should reassure them that you are dedicated to helping each other to discover the solutions. This kind of team functioning not only helps you feel supported but also strengthens your relationship.

Regarding several therapy options, be honest and transparent regarding their effectiveness. Important means of symptom control and overall improvement of quality of life are medications and therapy. For example, you could state that while therapy teaches people how to deal with their emotions when they change, drugs can help keep mood swings in control. Dealing with any concerns or misinterpretation they might have regarding their care is absolutely vital. If they are concerned about using medication or visiting a therapist, it is crucial to hear their worries and discuss them with them. Clear information and support regarding the advantages of these therapies will assist patients to overcome their worries and follow their treatment schedule.

Create a place where your teen feels secure expressing their emotions. Inquire of them to share their stories and pay attention to what they have to say. Think about their feelings and value what they are going through even if you do not completely know what they are going through. Saying words like "I can see why you might feel that way" or "That seems extremely tough" will help you to express that you respect their feelings rather than trying to solve the problem.

Remember that these conversations are meant to comfort and reassure your teen as well as to help them to see things in perspective. It entails beginning a dialogue in which they feel heard and understood so they may be free to discuss their illness and treatment. By keeping in touch and providing regular assistance, you can help your teen with bipolar illness feel safer and less alone.

Anticipate chats that never stop. Managing bipolar disease calls for constant communication rather than a one-time chat. As their circumstances change, your teen's questions and concerns might also alter. Frequent check-ins can help to maintain open lines of contact and ensure that they feel supported during their travel. Keep current with bipolar disease and the various therapies as well. More knowledge can help you to better assist your teen and handle any issues that arise.

By means of honest, open, and sympathetic chats, you can assist your teen in comprehending their issue and feel better about handling it. This kind of care not only helps them get better but also strengthens your bond with them, which facilitates their handling of the challenges related to bipolar disease.

Listening and Understanding Your Teen's Feelings

Really listening to your teen with bipolar illness and grasping what they are saying will be among the most crucial things you can do for them. Although managing bipolar illness might be challenging at times, it is rather vital to provide your teen a safe environment where they may share their emotions. Your teen will open up and discuss what is on their mind if you approach them fully attentively, sensitive, and kindly.

Make sure your teen's speech comes first if they express they wish to talk. Setting down your phone and turning off the TV may help you eliminate outside disturbances that might hinder your ability to concentrate on what they are saying. Meeting their gaze indicates that you are attentive and eager in what they have to offer. Paying attention to their tale can help you to demonstrate your interest in what they have to say and not only in listening.

Active listening is more than just avoiding chatting over your teen when they are speaking. Another aspect of the process is picking up nonverbal, nonphysical signals indicating someone is listening. Nod your head or say something like "I get it" or "Keep going" to indicate they should keep talking. Saying phrases like "I can see why you are feeling that way" or "That sounds extremely hard" will help you additionally convey your concern for their emotions. If you employ these lines, teenagers will know that you are more concerned in knowing their feelings than in merely mimicking what they say. Teenagers who experience bipolarity should realize that their illness might cause them to feel alone, so their feelings are appreciated and understood.

Let your teen complete what they are saying without stopping them to be the best thing you can do. Before you offer someone help or your own ideas, you should truly pay attention to what other people are saying and worried about. Sometimes it would be rather beneficial to be able to discuss issues without feeling as though you have to find solutions. You should not strive to solve their issues immediately on demand. Rather, you should be there for them, know what they are going through, and pay attention when they most need it.

During these conversations, it is rather crucial to acknowledge and help your teen with her emotions. Whether you agree with what they say or believe they are lying, it is crucial to realize their emotions are real. One could respond, "I see why you are unhappy" or "That must have been a rough time." These words indicate that you value your teen's opinion even if you disagree with them. This helps you to show them that you are there to assist them rather than to dismiss their issues.

Teenagers with bipolar illness particularly need this kind of care since they experience emotions more intensely than their peers. Their mood swings and great emotional highs and lows make them feel alone, hence it could be difficult for them to believe that anyone truly understands them. Showing your teen that you understand and are there for them will help them to feel less isolated in their circumstances. They will be aware that, despite their too powerful emotions, you will pay great attention.

These lengthy discussions foster confidence by means of their endurance. teenagers who believe you value what they have to say and are striving to understand them will be far more likely to chat to you going forward.

They may begin to distance themselves from you if they believe you constantly make decisions without consulting them or that you do not give any thought to their feelings. You want to strike a decent balance between truly listening and offering guidance. Your teen may simply want you to be there for them, not always to fix their problems but rather to listen and demonstrate your concern.

Recall that seeing is a daily activity. If your teen has bipolar illness, their everyday activities, mental health, and emotions could all vary greatly. One minute they can prefer to be alone and then need a lot of conversation from other people. Your teen will benefit from your awareness of these developments and sympathetic response. When they are ready to participate, let them lead; then, be patient and forgiving.

Recall that listening to someone does not automatically make you agree with them. Teenagers can be argumentative; occasionally you could even believe they are fabricating stuff. In any event, you need not experience the same feelings others do to grasp them. "I get how you feel right now, but I would like to discuss what happened tomorrow". This encourages constant communication and provides opportunities for individuals to grasp and fix issues as needed.

More than just listening to what your bipolar teen says is required to truly pay attention to them. Knowing that you will always be there for them and never criticize them, the objective is for them to feel safe enough to share with you their emotions. If you are patient, kind, and totally present with your teen while they negotiate the ups and downs of bipolar illness, you and them will develop closer and feel more supported.

How You Can Handle Difficult Conversations About Treatment and Safety with your teen

Especially if your teen is battling with bipolar disease, managing challenging talks about treatment and safety with them can feel overwhelming. Though they might be emotionally charged and difficult, these conversations are vital for their well-being. Topics like routinely taking medicine, controlling dangerous actions during manic periods, and addressing self-harm or suicide ideas during depressed phases call for careful, sympathetic treatment combined with a clear plan in mind.

Having these talks starts with you staying cool and collected. Your teen will probably sense your emotions, hence if you approach the subject with terror or rage, they might react defensively or shut down. Although the subjects under discussion are weighty, maintaining a cool head can help foster a more honest and open conversation. This also establishes the tone in which you are here to help them—not to criticize or counsel them. Remember, you want to be someone they can turn to for safety—not someone they feel they should keep their difficulties secret.

Regarding therapy and safety, one should be direct. You want to avoid sugar-coating the gravity of the matter as doing so can cause misinterpretation of the need to follow their treatment course. When talking about medication, for instance, fully explain why it is crucial to follow directions exactly and how missing doses could compromise their mood stability. Tell the truth about the results of deviating from the treatment plan, but steer clear of seeming as though the talk is a lecture. You want them to comprehend, not to make them feel guilty or corrected.

Using "I" rather than "you" words helps you to approach these talks without making your teen defensive. Saying, "I am genuinely concerned about your safety," feels less accusing than saying, "You never take your prescription seriously." The "I" phrase reveals that instead of blaming your emotions on anything, you are expressing them. Your teen's response can change significantly depending on this little linguistic change. It creates the path for a more sympathetic dialogue instead of making them feel cornered or guilty.

When dealing with dangerous behaviors, such impulsive actions during manic episodes, you should approach your teen in a way that makes them feel supported instead of judged. You might explain, "I observed that you seem to be more prone to take risks during your manic periods. How that might compromise your safety worries me. This not only notes their actions but also shows that you care about their welfare, thereby indicating that you wish to help rather than punish them.

Talking about ideas of self-harm or suicide—which can be quite challenging but extremely vital—is another vital subject. Whether your teen shares these ideas or not, you should treat them extremely seriously regardless of their casual or offhanded nature. Saying something like, Tell your teen there is help available and that these emotions are nothing to be embarrassed of. Remind them they are not alone in their difficulties and encourage them to be honest about their emotions.

Should your teen express ideas of self-harm or suicide, quick response is needed to guarantee their safety. Eliminate any possible sources of injury, including drugs, sharp objects, or anything else that might be used. Although this seems like a big step, it is essential to avoid acting impulsively at very emotional times. Once their immediate safety has been confirmed, assist their mental health provider or, if needed, call emergency services to arrange for the required treatment. Tell them that seeking help is a necessary first step in asserting control of their mental health rather than a show of weakness.

Always finish all these challenging talks by stressing your love and encouragement. Tell your teen that your first focus is their health and happiness and that you are there for them no matter what. They have to realize you are on their side and that getting help is not something to run from or avoid.

Although these talks are difficult, they are absolutely vital in allowing your teen to properly control their bipolar illness. Approach every conversation patiently, sympathetically, and with understanding. Your teen may occasionally feel overwhelmed or defensive, but this is natural. If you can remain cool and encouraging, you will be able to guide her through trying circumstances. Talking candidly about treatment and safety will help your teen understand that their well-being comes first and that they always know they can count on you for direction and support.

Building a Strong, Trusting Relationship with Your Teen

Especially if your teen suffers with bipolar illness, one of the most crucial things you can do is establish a strong and trustworthy relationship with them. A strong relationship based on trust, respect, and understanding not only helps in treating their condition more successfully but also deepens the link between you and your teen thereby enabling them to feel protected, supported, and understood.

A trusting relationship's basis is constancy. This involves keeping your word to your teen on any promises you make. Keeping your word is essential whether it is something little like pledging to spend time with them over the weekend or something more like helping them make treatment decisions. Your teen learns they can trust you when you show them you can be relied upon. Particularly on challenging subjects like their mental health, this constancy helps to foster the confidence required for more honest communication.

Another crucial component of developing trust is establishing and preserving well defined limits. Having limits gives your teen steadiness; bipolar illness can cause mood swings. Talking about and agreeing on these limits—such as household rules, routines, or obligations—helps one to better appreciate why they exist. Stressing their freedom but also being available to guide them demonstrates that you are strong but fair with these limits. Being adaptable when necessary is just as vital, particularly if their mental problem causes more difficulties. Demonstrating your ability to change and pay attention to their demands helps to build mutual respect.

Also very important is honoring your teen's right to privacy. Teenagers naturally yearn for autonomy; when bipolar illness strikes their life, they may feel even more compelled to exercise control over their own space and thoughts. Give them that time, but let them know you are always free to discuss when they feel ready. Sometimes it is better to let people share when they are comfortable than to force them to open on your timeline. Just being present offers them the choice.

One very effective approach to relate to your teen is by sharing your own challenges and experiences. Even if your experiences might differ from theirs, sharing your difficulties with them will help them to realize they are not alone in confronting trying circumstances. It is about demonstrating that everyone handles difficulties rather than about comparing hardships; it is good to ask for support. Your teen may feel less alone and more connected depending on this sensitivity.

Developing trust also depends on appreciating and rewarding your teen's efforts and successes—especially in terms of managing their illness. Exhaustive and overpowering, bipolar disorder can also sometimes feel glacial in progress. Celebrating even little accomplishments—like following their treatment plan or effectively managing a mood episode—helps increase their confidence and drive. Recognizing these efforts helps your teen to feel important and supports the belief that their diligence is recognized.

Building trust also depends on involving your teen in choices regarding their treatment course. Involve teens in talks with their healthcare providers instead of prescribing what they should do; ask for their opinion when debating treatment choices. Having this sensation of control can be quite freeing, enabling individuals to be more involved in their treatment. Those who feel as active participants in their treatment plan are more likely to remain dedicated and favorable about the procedure.

Additionally improving your connection is teaching and using coping mechanisms alongside each other. Although mindfulness, meditation, or journaling are helpful methods for bipolar illness management, their efficacy increases especially when used in concert. If your teen observes you trying to teach them these abilities, it not only indicates your dedication to supporting them but also your respect for their mental health. Together, you offer a chance for bonding by engaging in these events and also set an example of good coping mechanisms they might apply all their lives.

Another crucial method you may show your teen support is by helping them pinpoint the causes of their mood swings. This can be noting their moods in a notebook or just chatting about how particular events, pressures, or surroundings make them feel. Once you have recognized these triggers, you may cooperate to create plans to either regulate or avoid them, therefore strengthening your emotional regulation.

Furthermore, controlling bipolar illness depends on a consistent daily schedule since it offers structure and predictability that could help to balance mood fluctuations. Promote good practices include frequent exercise, a balanced diet, and proper sleep, all of which can help greatly control mood. Help your teen to keep friendships and engage in activities they enjoy so supporting their social relationships. Social support is quite important; feeling connected to others can offer an emotional release apart from the family.

Developing a good, trustworthy relationship with your teen ultimately calls for time, work, and patience. You build a basis of support that will help them now and going forward by regularly showing up for them, honoring their needs, including them in their care, and recognizing their achievements. Although managing mental health is a lifetime endeavor, when done so with love, empathy, and teamwork, it will be a road that builds both of you.

Chapter 5

How You Can Take Care of Yourself and Find Support While Helping Your Teen

Parents may experience mental and physical fatigue from caring for an adolescent with bipolar disorder. Remember that you need to put your own needs first, even when your teen's needs are more pressing. The importance of building a support system, keeping a positive attitude on the future, finding support groups, cooperating with your teen's school, and parents' need for self-care are all topics covered in this chapter.

Why Parents Need to Take Care of Themselves Too

It is not easy to be a parent of a teen with bipolar illness. You and your teen could feel worn out and stressed given all the mood swings, erratic conduct, and emotional pressure. Let your needs come first, then your own self-care may be easy. Still, self-care is vital. Giving your demands top priority is not selfish; rather, it will help you to enable your teenage son.

Physical and emotional tiredness could make it more difficult to handle daily tasks including caring for an adolescent bipolar patient. Even little problems might seem like heavy loads when you are exhausted, and you will not be able to give your teen the calm direction, understanding, and patience they need. On the other hand, giving your own well-being first priority will help you to handle your teenage problems. It will sharpen your attitude, energy, and resilience.

Juggling family harmony, prescription tracking, and doctor's visits can make finding time for self-care seem impossible. Still, self-care does not have to involve planning a long trip or a fancy spa treatment. Little deeds could have a big influence. Effective ways to reset are reading a chapter from a book, going for a short walk outside, or turning on some music. After these quick but deliberate stops, you might find yourself feeling refreshed and relaxed. When you have time to heal, you can clearly and calmly manage difficult situations instead of becoming enraged and exhausted.

Realizing that one must first take care of oneself will help one to protect others. Attending your own mental and emotional well-being first will help you to be more able to help your teen. Self-care helps you to discover tranquility and positive energy, which will improve your connections with your teen and create a less demanding and more loving environment. If you can lower your stress, your teenager will most likely follow suit; this will help with communication and build your relationship.

Crucially, one should grow in self-compassion and understand that perfection is not required. Parents of teenagers with bipolar illness often find it somewhat normal and expected to know when their teens are struggling. Although parents are under great pressure to manage everything by themselves, asking for help shows strength rather than weakness. Making contact with family members or attending a support group for parents dealing with similar problems could be highly helpful. It assures you that you are not traveling alone and provides a stage for you to express your emotions, disappointments, and worries.

Having a support system helps you to rely on people when things are tough, so reducing the emotional stress. Through these contacts, you can get guidance and a sympathetic ear as well as practical help with errands and teen care. While raising a teen with bipolar illness is difficult, having encouraging people in your life makes a great impact.

Your mental and emotional well-being depends much on how you parent. You will find it challenging to meet your teen's demands in a patient and compassionate way if you are constantly tired, worried, or emotionally depleted. Your teen should see a positive example of the value of self-care. Teens with bipolar illness may struggle with emotional control, stress management, and keeping appropriate lifestyle choices including a balanced diet and enough sleep. Giving your own mental health top priority could help your teenage friend learn that it is acceptable and essential to look after oneself. They will see clearly that maintaining one's health calls for personal responsibility.

It could feel like a tightrope act, trying as you might to balance your needs with those of your teen. If you put yourself first, you could be worried that your teen will see less of you. Actually, though, giving your own needs top priority will free you to be more available and motivating to your teen when they most need you. Keeping the endurance and strength to meet the needs of your teen does not mean ignoring your own. Finding a good balance will help you and your teen avoid becoming overwhelmed by the challenges brought on by bipolar illness.

Knowing when to seek professional help is another absolutely important component of self-care. See a counselor or therapist to help you control strong emotions and situations. Coping strategies taught by mental health experts will enable you to control the emotional and psychological effects of looking after a teen with bipolar illness. It is fantastic that you are seeking help; you will benefit as well as your teen will. Finally, in addition to making time for oneself, self-care includes building the emotional resilience needed to be a great parent. Realizing that your own level of well-being greatly influences your capacity to help your adolescent on their mental health road map is vital. Making time for relaxation, regeneration, and getting treatment when needed guarantees that you have the tools to help your teenage friend manage the challenges related with bipolar illness. An active and rested parent is the best type of help available to an adolescent suffering with bipolar illness.

How to Find Help from Support Groups

Parents of teenagers with bipolar illness often find great benefit from getting in touch with support groups. Anxiety and loneliness are natural emotions; occasionally you could feel as though no one else can connect to your circumstances. Knowing that you are not alone in your problems could help you find comfort in a support group. Joining one of these organizations allows you to network with other parents who have gone through the same events as yours. Tell others about your difficulties and hear about your own to get great comfort. Reminding parents that other parents go through similar issues will help them to feel less isolated.

Parent support groups seek to provide a safe setting where parents may feel supported and understandingly treated. These forums give you a secure venue to share your goals, fears, and challenges. From everyday management of your teenage bipolar disorder symptoms to negotiating interactions with colleges, physicians, and other apparently impossible spheres of life, everyone here is aware of the difficulties associated. Talking to others who are going through similar circumstances is for many the most comforting aspect of visiting a support group. Realizing that others have gone through similar events and come out stronger can help you to keep on even if it requires bravery.

These groups not only give moral support but also often valuable direction and advice. Those whose parents have experienced bipolar illness for a significant period of time could be able to provide useful tips and strategies. Support group material can be quite useful for finding the correct doctors, controlling medication, and arranging suitable school accommodations. Learning about the successful techniques other parents use can inspire you to attempt something different with your teen, such as changing daily activities or applying fresh methods of controlling mood swings. The group's shared knowledge will help you to understand your teenager's treatment choices and negotiate the complex healthcare system.

Support groups have one major benefit in that they may point you toward services you might not have found on your own. Many companies provide speakers from these fields together with information on nearby mental health facilities, instructional materials, and families affected by bipolar illness programs. You might also look at possible family resources including books, websites, and counseling theories. By means of this network of services, you can obtain essential knowledge about professional help and the optimal therapeutic approaches for your teenage. These get-togethers provide moral support as well as useful skills that would help to ensure a more smooth travel experience.

Starting an online forum or in-person group is a great way to develop your sense of community. In-person meetings let parents personally interact and create lifelong connections that support closer ties. Excellent for building friendships, these get-togethers—which take place in places like hospitals, community centers, or schools—allow people to routinely connect with one another. Online groups are a great substitute if your location or schedule make it difficult for you to make in-person meeting attendance. With so many internet resources at hand, parents all around can easily be connected. Among a few are forums, online support groups, and social media groups. This adaptability makes it easy to choose a group that fits your calendar whether your desired attendance frequency is once a week or occasionally for extra help.

Attending a support group could help your teen as well as yourself. More parental support will help you to be more suited to help your teen. Talking to those who understand your circumstances and sharing your achievements will enable you to help them better manage the difficulties presented by bipolar illness. Having a parent less withdrawn and more adept in handling their illness will help your teen.

A sign of strength rather than weakness is asking help from a support group. Parents that feel they should be able to manage things on their own are reluctant to join organizations. Having said that, you should not feel compelled to take care of every problem or bear full responsibility for the development of your teen. Support groups are supposed to provide members a safe forum to share their issues, confide in one another, and get direction. Apart from looking after yourself, you can help your teen more successfully by depending on the support of other parents.

Collaborating with Your Teen's School

Together, you and the school your teen attends can assist them in managing their bipolar illness. How your teen interacts with teachers, guidance counselors, and other school staff determines their health and happiness. First thing parents should do to ensure their teen receives the required assistance is to establish close ties with the institution.

Talk first about your teen's bipolar illness in an honest and open manner with school personnel. The school has to know about your teen's circumstances regardless of how awkward it would be for you to divulge intimate knowledge. Among others, you should tell the clinician, guidance counselor, and school nurse your teen's diagnosis, symptoms, and probable reasons. Employees will then be ready to support your teen and steer clear of any potentially tense circumstances. Details are important; for example, how your teen controls their daily energy level and how their mood influences their behavior or focus. Keeping these issues open could allow the school to establish a conducive environment.

Working with the school to create a documented plan can allow you to ensure that your teen is receiving the necessary support. Many institutions provide choices including 504 Plans and Individualized Education Programs (IEPs). These are specialist courses covering mental disorders including bipolar disease. Your teen could be able to take breaks amid trying circumstances, have extra time on tests, or have access to a quiet study area. These could be included into an Individualized Education Program (IEP) or a 504 Plan. If teenagers apply these strategies, they can improve from their condition and perform well in their studies. Your teen will have the skills they need to excel in the classroom thanks to this schedule you and the institution created together.

Tell them what causes your teen's symptoms and how they handle them; this will assist the school in handling the issue. Teenagers with bipolar illness may experience extreme anxiety attacks while under stress over tasks, tests, or social events. If your teen struggles with concentration, mood swings, or acts without thinking, they may behave differently in the classroom. Should the institution notify staff members and teachers ahead of time, they will be able to create the suitable solutions for these issues. If your teen seems stressed or overstimulated in class, it could be beneficial for them to go outside for some time to cool down. Your teen will be more understanding and supported if you assist them in preparing ahead of time for these occasions.

Just as vital as attending to their social and psychological needs is helping your teen with their academics. Your teen can seek treatment from school psychologists or counselors should they be experiencing social or mental issues. Teenagers' mental health may be much improved by having a friend at their school who understands. In counseling sessions your teen visits, they can acquire good coping mechanisms and feel secure sharing their issues. You might propose setting up peer support groups or mental health awareness campaigns at the school so that every teen feels welcome and included in the betterment of the place.

Talking to the guidance counselors and teachers of your teen will enable you to determine the degree of effectiveness of their support system. Daily conversations with your teen will help you to learn about their mental health as well as their academic performance. Maintaining contact between both sides helps to settle issues promptly and enable any required modifications to the 504 Plan or Individualized Education Program (IEP). Your teen's needs could evolve with time, thus you should often review the plan to make sure it is still fit for them. As your teen grows and their health shifts, you might have to make some adjustments. The first tweaks could be successful. The greatest approach to ensure your teen receives the required assistance during their academic career is active participation.

Working with the school is not one-time; rather, it is a continuous process. Although they might be able to assist your teen, teachers and officials might not fully comprehend bipolar disease. When this occurs, you should defend your teen and request additional school assistance or information. Although schools want to be of assistance, they could also want greater knowledge on how to assist a bipolar student. Working together among all those engaged in your teen's education guarantees that everyone is in agreement.

Finally, keep in mind that developing a relationship with the school starts with gathering a group of individuals to back your teen. Giving your teen additional test time and counselor access will help them; but, you also have to make sure they feel understood, comfortable, and capable of success. Regularly talking to each other and working together will help your teen manage their bipolar illness and homework. This support will enable them to learn how to manage several aspects of their sickness, feel better about themselves, and perform better in class.

Following these guidelines and getting active will help your teen deal with their bipolar illness and have the best possibility to perform well in school. Meeting your teen's intellectual, social, and emotional requirements can help them grow into a confident and capable young adult.

Building a Support System of Family and Friends

Raising a teen with bipolar illness calls for a network of family and friends surrounding you. You are not traveling this road alone, hence having a solid network would be quite beneficial for you in handling your challenges. Family and close friends can provide you both emotional and physical support, easing the daily weight you bear.

Start by contacting those you know you can rely upon. Among these could be a close friend who knows you well, an aunt or uncle, or a relative. Share with them the issues your teen is presenting to you. People do not usually volunteer since they are unsure of your needs. By sharing your predicament with them, you allow them an opportunity to assist you.

Very beneficial are family and friends who are there for you emotionally. Having someone to chat to can help you relax when you are overwhelmed or anxious. Sometimes all you need is to talk about how you feel; you never always need guidance or assistance. Talking to someone you trust about your issues will enable you to remember that you are not alone and get through the daily challenges.

Having folks close by can also be rather beneficial in actual terms. Ask for help if you need a break or if you have running duties. Someone might, for instance, monitor your teen for a few hours while you are away from her. You could feel better even from little deeds of kindness like cleaning the house or gathering your food. When you ask for help, you have more time to concentrate on both your teen's needs and your own self-care, both of which are really critical.

Knowing more about bipolar disease will help your family and friends assist you and your teen more effectively. Many individuals would not really understand what bipolar illness is or how it would influence your family. Spend some time discussing bipolar illness and how it influences your teen's mood and conduct. You can also assist them in several spheres. People you care about can help you more profoundly if they better grasp your position.

Talking about the indicators of mood swings—such as extreme sadness or a lot of energy—you can help your teen identify whether she is struggling. You can also let them know how your teen might be helped during these times and what might trigger these episodes—stress from school or social events. More will benefit you from friends and relatives if they know more.

Having friends and relatives assist you in caring for your teen will also help to improve the environment for them. When times are tough, for example, grandparents or other close relatives can be a consistent and caring presence that offers assistance. Friends and family may also provide your teen with appropriate coping mechanisms for difficult situations so they may grow in emotional control. Having loving adults around your teen will help them to feel more supported and safer.

Over time, a robust support structure will also benefit your teen and yourself. As your teen develops and confronts fresh challenges, having a network of individuals who know her needs can be quite beneficial. Those who have been there from the start will be familiar with your teen's requirements and will be able to support them through many phases of life, including those when they begin a career or college.

Remember that creating a support group proceeds in both directions. As with your own needs, you can also assist friends and relatives when they require it. Supporting one another strengthens bonds and fosters closer ties and confidence. It creates a network of people who can cooperatively manage the ups and downs of life, therefore simplifying everyone's path.

How to Stay Positive About the Future with your teen Bipolar disorder

Staying positive when you are looking after your teen helps you and them even if it can be challenging. Though it seems unattainable, maintaining a good attitude can truly assist. Many teenagers with bipolar illness go on to lead fulfilling, successful lives if they receive the appropriate therapy and help.

To keep hopeful, pay notice to the minor wins. If your teen follows their prescription exactly, visits a therapist, or even just has a day when their conditions allow, it is quite significant. These little victories will increase their confidence and assist them to feel better about their development.

Developing a habit could enable you to feel more grounded. Your teen will feel safer and more in control if you make sure they eat well, go to therapy as advised, and sleep at consistent times. Though things will not always go as intended, your best efforts to follow a schedule will help them go without incident.

Help your teen create and pursue their own goals. They might be about education, pastimes, or topics directly relevant to you. Helping them break out these goals into smaller, more realistic steps could help them appear less frightening. Celebrate their accomplishments and be there for them should they run across difficulties while they travel. Encourage them to keep focused on their objectives so as to inspire and motivate them.

Another benefit is establishing relationships with those experiencing the same circumstances. Parents of teenagers with bipolar disease can find aid, share their tales, and feel as though they are understood by means of support groups. Speaking with someone who knows what you are going through will help you feel better and provide you with smart solutions for handling the illness of your teen.

You should also keep in contact with the nurses and doctors seeing your teen. Regular visits to their doctor or therapist will help your teen confirm whether their treatment is working. They can assist in modifying their course of treatment if so needed. If you can communicate effectively with these professionals, you will be more sure about looking after your teen and experience peace of mind.

You have to take care of yourself as much as you do of your teen. Taking care of a teen with bipolar disease can be difficult, thus plan rest and recuperation time.. Taking care of your own needs—that of performing activities you enjoy, working out, or spending time with loved ones—helps you stay well and more suited to support your teen.

Ask for help without hesitation if you so need it. Talking to a counselor or therapist is a great approach to handle the tension and emotions of caring for someone. Support and practical assistance might also come from family and friends. Having a solid network of individuals that love you helps you to remain strong and cheerful.

Your teen should fantasize about the future and put great effort toward achieving their objectives. Finding those who have effectively managed bipolar illness can inspire you. Your hope for their future will truly motivate them to perform at their best. Setting goals, following a schedule, emphasizing minor wins, attending support groups, keeping in touch with doctors, and looking after yourself will help your teen create a decent environment. Recall that many things and individuals could be of use to you.

The Conclusion

Raising a teen with bipolar illness is a road full of opportunities as well as obstacles. Though at times the future seems unknown, it is important to hang on to the hope that your teen can lead a meaningful and successful life given the appropriate help and therapy.

Living with bipolar illness could be frightening for your teen. One can feel overwhelmed by the mood swings, unpredictability, and necessity of ongoing management of their disease. Still, many young people with bipolar illness develop into strong adults who learn to negotiate their emotions and difficulties. Correct treatment—including therapy and medication—allows them to create a life full of personal accomplishments, close relationships, and a feeling of purpose.

The future of your teen presents great possibilities for achievement and development. Though they may have setbacks, every stride forward—no matter how little—attests to their bravery and fortitude. Their family, friends, and medical team's support can make a big impact. Encouragement of your teen to follow their aspirations and passions as well as to help them control their condition creates optimism and possibilities.

Parentally, one is naturally worried about the future. The mental and physical toll of providing care can be great. Still, your teen's foundation for a positive future is being built by you in great measure. Powerful instruments on their path are your love, patience, and unflinching support. Your teen can flourish in a supportive atmosphere you help establish by keeping educated and interested.

Looking ahead, one should not forget that possibilities for both difficulties and successes abound in the future. You are laying the groundwork for a better future by concentrating on the positive actions you can do right now—such as controlling therapy, creating a solid support system, and engaging in self-care.

You and your teen can boldly and deliberately confront the future. Although the road may be difficult, the love and encouragement you offer will enable your teen to confidently and resiliently negotiate their path. Accepting this optimistic viewpoint helps your teen as well as improves your capacity to be there for them through the highs and lows of their illness.

Your path as a parent speaks to your will and commitment. Though the route may be difficult, every effort you make helps clear the path for a day when your teen may enjoy a happy, fulfilled life. With ongoing support, empathy, and care, hold on to the hope that the future can present many happy, successful, and growth-oriented events for your teen and yourself.